# A Catholic Child's First
# Book of Prayers

# A Catholic Child's First Book of Prayers

Catholic™
CLASSICS

Edited by
*REV. VICTOR HOAGLAND, C.P.*

Illustrations by
*WILLIAM LUBEROFF*

Regina
Press

Imprimatur:
C. Eykens, Vic. gen.
Antverpiae, 6 junii 1986

THE REGINA PRESS
10 Hub Drive
Melville, New York
www.reginapress.com

ISBN# 9780882713649

Printed in China.

# IMPORTANT PRAYERS

## The Sign of the Cross

In the name of the Father
and of the Son
and of the Holy Spirit. Amen.

## The Lord's Prayer

Our Father, who art in heaven,
hallowed be Thy name;
Thy kingdom come;
Thy will be done on earth
as it is in heaven.
Give us this day
our daily bread;
and forgive us our trespasses
as we forgive those
who trespass against us
and lead us not into temptation,
but deliver us from evil. Amen.

## The Hail Mary

Hail Mary, full of grace,
the Lord is with thee.
Blessed art thou among women,
and blessed is the fruit of thy womb, Jesus.
Holy Mary, Mother of God, pray for us
sinners, now and at the hour of our death.
Amen.

## Glory Be

Glory be to the Father,
and to the Son,
and to the Holy Spirit,
as it was in the beginning,
is now, and ever shall be,
world without end. Amen.

# The Apostles' Creed

I believe in God the Father Almighty, Creator of heaven and earth; and in Jesus Christ, His only Son, our Lord; who was conceived by the Holy Spirit, born of the Virgin Mary, suffered under Pontius Pilate, was crucified, died, and was buried; He descended into hell; the third day He rose again from the dead; He ascended into heaven, and is seated at the right hand of God the Father almighty; from thence He shall come to judge the living and the dead. I believe in the Holy Spirit; the holy Catholic Church; the Communion of Saints; the forgiveness of sins; the resurrection of the body; and life everlasting. Amen.

# Act of Contrition

O my God,
I am heartily sorry
for having offended You,
and I detest all my sins,
because of Your just punishments,
and most of all
because they offend You, my God,
who are good
and deserving of all my love.
I firmly resolve,
with the help of Your grace
to sin no more
and to avoid the near occasions
of sin. Amen.

# Act of Faith

O my God, I believe that You are one God in three Divine Persons: Father, Son and Holy Spirit. I believe that Your Divine Son became Man and died for our sins, and that He will come again to judge the living and the dead. I believe these and all truths that the Catholic Church teaches, because You have revealed them, who can neither deceive nor be deceived. Amen.

## Act of Hope

O my God, relying on Your almighty power and infinite mercy and promises, I hope to obtain pardon of my sins, the help of Your grace and life everlasting through the merits of Jesus Christ, my Lord and Redeemer. Amen.

## Act of Love

O my God, I love You above all things with my whole heart and soul, because You are all good and worthy of all love. I love my neighbors as myself for the love of You. I forgive all who have injured me and ask pardon of all whom I have injured. Amen.

# PRAYER TO MARY

## The Memorare

Remember, O most loving Virgin Mary, That never was it known that anyone who asked for your protection, or looked for your aid, or begged for your prayers, was left without help. As I think of this, I fly to you, O Virgin of Virgins, my Mother. To you I go, before you I kneel, filled with sorrow for my sins. Do not turn away for me, O Mother of Jesus, but hear me and pray for me to your son. Amen.

# PRAYER TO JESUS

## Soul of Christ

Soul of Christ, sanctify me,
Body of Christ, save me.
Blood of Christ, inebriate me.
Water from the side of Christ, wash me.

Passion of Christ, strengthen me.
O good Jesus, hear me.
Within your wounds, hide me.

Separated from you, let me never be.
From the malignant enemy, defend me.

At the hour of death, call me.
To come to You, bid me,
that I may praise You
in the company of Your saints,
for all eternity. Amen.

## A Morning Offering

◯ Jesus, I offer You everything
I shall do and say and think today.
I offer You my happy times
and my sad times.
I offer them so that all You want
may come to pass.
I join my prayers to those of Mary,
Your Mother, who is my mother,
too. Amen.

## Before Meals

Bless us, O Lord,
and these Your gifts,
which we are about to receive
from Your goodness,
Through Christ, our Lord.
May the Lord relieve the wants
of others. Amen.

## Nighttime Prayer

Matthew, Mark, Luke and John,
Bless the bed that I lie on.
Before I lay me down to sleep,
I give my soul to Christ to keep.
Four corners to my bed,
Four angels overhead:
One at the head, one at the feet,
And two to guard me while I sleep.
Amen.

# The Stations of The Cross

### First Station
### Jesus Is Condemned to Death

Jesus is brought before Pilate to be judged. He is innocent but he is condemned and taken away to be put to death.

### Second Station
### Jesus Takes Up His Cross

The cross is very heavy. Jesus knows it will be painful but He accepts it willingly to save us from our sins.

### Third Station
### Jesus Falls for the First Time

The heavy cross drives the thorns still deeper into His brow.  Jesus is weak from the loss of blood. He falls and the soldiers roughly drag Him up again.

## Fourth Station
## Jesus Meets His Mother

When Mary sees Jesus, her heart is broken.
He is covered with dirt and blood. Mary weeps
because He is  suffering terribly and there is no
way she can help Him.

## Fifth Station
## Simon of Cyrene Helps Jesus

Jesus is so weak He can no longer carry the
cross. The soldiers fear that He will faint or
die on the way. So they ask a man named
Simon to help Him.

## Sixth Station
## Veronica Wipes the Face of Jesus

A good lady runs to Jesus and wipes His
face with her veil. How she pitied Him and how
anxious she was to do something
for Him!

### Seventh Station
### Jesus Falls the Second Time

Again Jesus staggers under the weight of the cross and falls heavily to the ground. The cruel soldiers, with kicks and blows, force Him to His feet again.

### Eighth Station
### Jesus Meets the Women of Jerusalem

Jesus meets some women who are grieving and crying loudly. He tells them not to weep for Him but for all the sinners who will not repent and be saved.

### Ninth Station
### Jesus Falls the Third Time

Jesus is now near the place where He will be fastened to the cross. He thinks of all the pain He must still suffer. All His strength leaves Him and He falls to the earth.

## Tenth Station
### Jesus Is Stripped of His Clothes

The long journey to Calvary is now finished. The soldiers roughly tear off His clothes. Jesus is humiliated and treated like a common criminal.

## Eleventh Station
### Jesus Is Nailed to the Cross

At last, Jesus is placed upon the cross. The soldiers then drive nails through His hands and feet. The cross is then raised and placed into the earth.

## Twelfth Station
### Jesus Dies on the Cross

How patiently Jesus suffers. For three long hours His body hangs on the cross. He speaks kindly to the good thief. He lovingly talks to Mary. At last He bows His head and dies.

## Thirteenth Station
## The Body of Jesus
## Is Taken Down from the Cross

After His death, friends take Jesus down from the cross. Gently they lower His body into the arms of His mother, Mary. With great love she again holds her beloved son.

## Fourteenth Station
## The Body of Jesus
## Is Laid in the Tomb

The body of Jesus is placed in a tomb. Soldiers seal the tomb and block the entrance with a great stone. The followers of Jesus return to their homes to wait for Jesus to rise from the dead on the third day, as He promised.

## Prayer Before A Crucifix

Look down upon me, good and gentle Jesus, while before Your face I humbly kneel and with burning soul pray and beseech You to fix deep in my heart lively sentiments of faith, hope and charity, true contrition for my sins, a firm purpose of amendment.

While I contemplate, with great love and tender pity, Your five most precious wounds, pondering over them within me and calling to mind the words which David, Your prophet, said of You, my Jesus:

"They have pierced my hands and my feet, they have injured all my bones." Amen.

# THE ROSARY

The Rosary is made up of sets, or groups, of beads on a chain. In each set there is one big bead and ten small beads. Each set is called a decade.

On the big beads, we say the Our Father. On the small beads, we say the Hail Mary. After the last Hail Mary in a decade, we say a Glory Be. Before each decade, we think of something that happened to Jesus and Mary. The complete Rosary consists of 20 decades and is further divided into the Joyful, Luminous, Sorrowful and Glorious Mysteries.

## The Joyful Mysteries

1. The Annunciation
2. The Visitation
3. The Birth of Jesus
4. The Presentation of Jesus in the Temple
5. The Finding of Jesus in the Temple

## The Luminous Mysteries

1. The Baptism of Jesus
2. The Wedding at Cana
3. The Proclamation of the Kingdom of God
4. The Transfiguration
5. The Institution of the Holy Eucharist

## The Sorrowful Mysteries

1. The Agony in the Garden
2. The Scourging of Jesus
3. The Crowning of Jesus with Thorns
4. The Carrying of the Cross
5. The Death of Jesus on the Cross

## The Glorious Mysteries

1. The Resurrection
2. The Ascension
3. The Coming of the Holy Spirit
4. The Assumption of Mary
5. The Coronation of Mary in Heaven

# The Ten Commandments

1. I, the Lord, am your God. You shall not have other gods besides me.

2. You shall not take the name of the Lord, your God, in vain.

3. Remember to keep holy the sabbath day.

4. Honor your father and your mother.

5. You shall not kill.

6. You shall not commit adultery.

7. You shall not steal.

8. You shall not bear false witness against your neighbor.

9. You shall not covet your neighbor's wife.

10. You shall not covet anything that belongs to your neighbor.

# The Beatitudes

1. Blessed are the poor in spirit, for the kingdom of heaven is theirs.

2. Blessed are those who are sad, for they shall be comforted.

3. Blessed are the mild and gentle, for they shall inherit the land.

4. Blessed are those who hunger and thirst for justice, for they shall be filled.

5. Blessed are the merciful, for they shall receive mercy.

6. Blessed are the pure in heart, for they shall see God.

7. Blessed are those who make peace, for they shall be called the peacemakers.

8. Blessed are those who suffer for My sake, for heaven will be theirs.

# What the Church Asks of Us

1. That we go to Mass on Sundays and holy days of obligation.

2. That we fast and abstain on the days appointed.

3. That we confess our sins at least once a year.

4. That we receive Holy Communion during Easter time.

5. That we contribute to the support of the Church.

6. That we observe the laws of the Church on marriage.

# The Sacraments

*The seven sacraments are special ways established by Jesus to help us live God's life more fully. Each sacrament brings with it a special grace from God.*

*They are:*

1.   Baptism

2.   Confirmation

3.   Holy Eucharist

4.   Reconciliation

5.   Anointing of the Sick

6.   Holy Orders

7.   Matrimony

# Virtues
## God's Gifts to Us

Faith - we believe all that God tells us.

Hope - we trust that God will always help us.

Love - we love God and all people.

## Gifts of the Holy Spirit

Wisdom

Knowledge

Understanding

Piety

Counsel

Fear of the Lord

Fortitude

# The Chief Corporal Works of Mercy

To feed the hungry.

To give drink to the thirsty.

To clothe the naked.

To visit the imprisoned.

To shelter the homeless.

To visit the sick.

To bury the dead.

# The Chief Spiritual Works of Mercy

To admonish the sinner.

To instruct the ignorant.

To counsel the doubtful.

To comfort the sorrowful.

To bear wrongs patiently.

To forgive all injuries.

To pray for the living and the dead.